REAL

Life

Takes Guts

GO FOR IT!

Jim Auer

Liguori

ONE LIGUORI DRIVE
LIGUORI MO 63057-9999
314.464.2500

Imprimi Potest:
Richard Thibodeau, C.SS.R.
Provincial, Denver Province
The Redemptorists

Imprimatur:
Most Reverend Michael J. Sheridan
Auxiliary Bishop, Archdiocese of St. Louis

ISBN 0-7648-0186-4
Library of Congress Catalog Card Number: 97-74318

Copyright © 1998, Jim Auer
Printed in the United States of America
98 99 00 01 02 5 4 3 2 1

The material in this booklet first appeared in slightly different form in *Liguorian* magazine.

Scripture quotations are from the *New Revised Standard Version of the Bible*, copyright © 1989 by the Division of Christian Education of the National Council of the Churches of Christ in the U.S.A. Used with permission. All rights reserved.

Scripture quotations in Chapter 2 (Proverbs 21:6 and Proverbs 11:1) are from the *New American Bible*, copyright © 1970, 1986, and 1991 by the Confraternity of Christian Doctrine, 3211 Fourth Street N.E., Washington, DC 20017-1194, and are used with permission. All rights reserved.

Bohemian Rhapsody, words and music by Freddie Mercury © 1975 B. Feldman & Co., Ltd., trading as Trident Music. All rights controlled and administered by Glenwood Music Corp. All rights reserved. International copyright secured. Used by permission.

Cover design by Christine Kraus

Contents

Chapter One Half (1/2)

Sex, Drugs, Rock and Roll, and the Loch Ness Monster

Author: Caught you.

Reader: Doing what?

Author: Reading this book.

Reader: Okay, I'll stop. I'll never do it again. I've kicked the habit. I'll put the book—

Author: No, *wait!* It's okay. I was just kidding. If you stop reading, we can't have this conversation.

Reader: Some conversation.

Author: Okay, it's a little different, but I think it's important.

Reader: Why?

Author: Because sometimes it's good to ease into a book, slip into it gradually, with a little advance information. Especially a book like this, a book about moral issues. Sometimes that phrase can be misleading.

Reader: I thought it was pretty clear. The book is about sex, drugs, explicit rock and roll, and the magic word for all of them is "*NO!*" Am I right?

Author: Not exactly.

Reader: I can't believe you're going to say "Yes" to all those things.

Author: That's why we need this conversation. Remember 2 + 2 = 4?

Reader: Rings a bell.

Author: It's an automatic reaction, and of course it's correct. Well, something like that happens with "teens" and "moral issues." Everyone figures, "Teens + Moral issues = Sex and Drugs." But that's *not* completely correct.

Reader: Aren't those moral issues?

Author: Sure they are. Major ones. And handling them badly can—well, look around and see the casualty count. That's why I said "not completely." The point is, those aren't the only moral issues. Actually, they flow out of some broader, more basic ideas.

Reader: Like what?

Author: Like, what does it mean to be free? Or the idea of getting away with something "as long as nobody's getting hurt." We'll start by talking about some of those broader ideas.

Reader: A couple questions. First, the title of this chapter: What's the Loch Ness monster got to do with any of this?

Author: Besides the fact that I *like* the Loch Ness monster, some people look at God, faith, right, and wrong the way they look at the Loch Ness monster: maybe there is such a thing, maybe not, and what difference does it make? That's sad. They make *all* the difference.

Reader: Last question. Why did you call this "Chapter One Half?" Why didn't you call it the Introduction?

Author: How many books have you read?

Reader: Quite a few.

Author: How many times have you skipped the Introduction?

Reader: I get the point. You're a little sneaky.

Author: But otherwise very lovable. That's straight out of real life, by the way; my wife says so.

Reader: She's got guts.

Chapter One

Are We Free or Not?

MICRO QUIZ

___ Freedom is
A) just a big myth, especially when you're young
B) just a big myth, especially when you're older
C) a right and a total reality for everyone
D) a wonderful and dangerous gift

(ANSWER AT END OF CHAPTER)

Now the Lord is the Spirit, and *where the Spirit of the Lord is*, there is freedom.
2 Corinthians 3:17

As servants of God, live as free people, yet do not use your freedom as a pretext for evil.
1 Peter 2:16

I'm sorry, but I get really depressed talking about freedom, so pardon me if I'm not my usual bright and breezy self. I get depressed talking about freedom because I'm not really very free.

I used to think that when I reached this age, I'd be calling my own shots. When you're young, other people set rules for you, and that's okay. But now that I'm fifty-fi—now that I'm about to begin middle age, I figured I'd be in total charge of my life.

What a joke! To start with, I have to be in my classroom by 7:45—*in the morning!* What if I wake up tired? Can I call my principal and say I'll be in around ten? Of course not.

I'd like to see a movie tonight, and I guess I'm *kind of* free to do that but not totally. For example, I'll have to pay to get in, and they charge way too much, even for a great film like *Robocop and Lassie vs. the Slime*.

Speaking of money, that's another way I'm not free. I don't get to keep all the money I make because of income tax. Income tax is money you give the government to come up with stuff we could probably take care of perfectly well by ourselves or else do without, like highways, national security, and so on. If you don't pay your income tax, they send a platoon of highly trained government agents after you. When the agents catch you, you have to pay your tax plus a fine, and you have to write, "I will never be nasty to my sweet, lovable Internal Revenue Service again" a thousand times.

And they call this a free country.

That's…not exactly a mature approach to freedom. It's also not how I *truly* think and feel, although there are times when a touch of it runs through my emotional veins. But we can use it as a springboard to think about freedom.

Wonderful and strange thing, freedom. We long for it and talk about it and celebrate it in the United States on the Fourth of July. But freedom is still mysterious; understanding it requires some work.

Take the job, for example. This is a free country, true. But I still have to show up for work tomorrow. Well, it depends on what you mean by "have to." If I sleep in, no state police will break down my door, put me in chains, drag me to the classroom, point guns at my head, and shout, "Teach linking verbs or die!" But if I want to keep my job, there's this old custom of showing up and doing it. It's more than an old custom. It's the only way life can work.

Maybe it's different in heaven. Maybe a heavenly "day" begins whenever I want, ends whenever I want, and is full only of things I want to do, including nothing. But this is earth. If I try to get into Total Heavenly Freedom Mode while I'm still in Cincinnati, I'll make myself (and other people whose lives touch mine in various ways) pretty miserable and upset.

"Freedom is a myth, an illusion," a student of mine complained once. "We say we're free, but we're not."

He was looking at freedom from that Absolutely-No-Obligations point of view. In that sense, it's an illusion all right. No such thing.

Which is a good deal. If our freedom were never restricted in any way by anything whatsoever, or if we never accepted those restrictions, most of the great, wonderful things that happen on this planet would never happen. Maybe none of them would ever happen. Why?

Anything we do that is worthwhile restricts our freedom in some way.

Soccer, for example, greatly restricts your freedom. If you want to play, you have to spend time going to practices, conditioning your body, and then showing up for games—on time. When you get there, you have to play by the rules, like "No tripping," even though it might be a great way to steal the ball.

"But that's different. People *want* to play soccer."

But you're not likely to find a soccer player who goes into a frenzy of joy and fulfillment over every session of practice. Sometimes it's fun, sometimes it's a little slow, and sometimes it's a real drag, even if you basically like soccer. But soccer is a package deal, and if you want it, you take the package, including the restrictions on your freedom.

Relationships are another example—friendship, going together, marriage, parenthood, almost any kind of relationship. Relationships gobble up freedom like the Cookie Monster in a warehouse of cookies.

They take time. Often it's time we willingly, eagerly give—but not always. When you're jolted awake at two in the morning by a five-month-old baby's cry from across the hall, you do not jump out of bed thinking, *Cool! I have this great opportunity to stop sleeping, get up, and feed the kid! This will be a thrill! Maybe if I'm lucky, it'll happen again at four-thirty!*

But you do it. If you walk to the crib and deliver a Freedom-for-Parents-to-Sleep! speech, your kid will not be impressed. If you want the child, you get the package. The package comes labeled, "A lot of restrictions on your freedom will apply." Most packages do, and almost everything in life comes as a package.

Besides being wonderful and strange and a basic right, freedom is also a dangerous gift. A little fantasy might help us understand that.

Imagine yourself as a parent with several children. That's probably not reality yet, but it's not total fantasy either. Here comes the fantasy: imagine that you are able to give your children the gift of flight.

Yes, flight. Not in airplanes or helicopters, but with their own bodies in a wonderful, thrilling canceling of gravity. Imagine that all parents are able to give this gift to their children.

Obviously it would be fun, but they could also do wonderful things with this gift. People caught on the third or even thirtieth floor of a burning building could escape with no problem. Naturalists trying to determine how many bald eagle or spotted owl nests are left would have an easier job and a more accurate count. Friends could visit one another more easily and more often. More people would come to important meetings (getting out of the house and to the meeting is usually half the hassle) to do the work of the city or the parish or the youth group or whatever they're involved in. With a little imagination, you can think of dozens of other examples.

But this gift could have a dark side, too. People could get away with burglary far more easily. It would be easier to skip school, too. Or run— fly away from home. Or simply spend too much time flying for the fun of it and not enough time doing things that need to be done. It would be easy to fly too far and get lost. It would be easy to fly too high or try stupid stunts in the air.

All kinds of bad things, along with all the good things, could happen because of this wonderful ability and gift.

That's exactly what happened when God made us free. That's what happened when God created us with the ability to make decisions, to choose.

Freedom means that another person can give you a hug, a compliment, a check for a thousand dollars, a piece of good advice, a slap in the face, a knife in the gut, or a bullet in the heart. You can do the same.

It wouldn't have to be that way. God could have made it so that we could do only good things. Either we would never think of doing anything wrong, or God would stop us anytime we were considering it. Think of all the trouble, all the suffering, all the heartache that would prevent.

God took a huge cosmic gamble by making us free, so there must be a reason for it. There is. God fell in love with us. God fell in love with the idea of us even before we were made. But not even God can fall in love with a robot, a clever mechanism with a computer chip for a soul.

Try it yourself. Build a realistic-looking humanoid contraption, and program it to walk up to you, give you a mechanical hug, and say that it loves you and thinks you're wonderful. You might feel good about your inventive genius, but you don't feel warm, wonderful, and accepted—and you're definitely not in love. You can program the thing to say "I love you" a thousand times a week, but you'll never feel loved. It won't mean anything except that you're a clever inventor of *things*.

It's the same with us and God. God doesn't want robots. They're handy, but they're things, not people. God loves and wants to be loved in return. Love requires freedom, the ability to choose to love.

But freedom is like a coin. If you're going to have a coin at all, it's going to have two sides. You can print the same thing on each side, but it still has two sides. No such thing as a coin with only one side. Same with freedom: if you're free to do wonderful things, you have to be free to do awful things. Otherwise it's not freedom.

Bottom lines on freedom: It's wonderful. It's mysterious. It's what makes us specifically human instead of nicely developed apes. It gives meaning to our actions. But it's dangerous, too.

And it's not total. *As soon as you're involved with other people, you give up part of the freedom to do what you want on your own sweet schedule.* The total freedom that some people dream about would exist only on an island inhabited by one person who somehow did not have to do a single thing even for food or shelter.

Sound good? Well maybe for a day or so. After that it sounds pretty lonely and boring. Another free human being on the island with you would help. But then you'd need to spend time with that person, including times when you would prefer to be alone. There would be occasions when that person would need you, and they wouldn't happen only when you wanted to be needed. There would be times when something you wanted conflicted with something the other person had a right to.

In the end, we're free to do anything we want—or at least give it a shot—as long as it doesn't violate someone else's rights (including God's!) or harm someone (including ourselves).

That covers a countless number of things.

It's a good idea to say thanks for the beautiful gift of freedom and ask for the good judgment to use it wisely. We can do horrible harm when we don't—and enormous good when we do.

"ANSWER" TO MICRO QUIZ

A   If you chose this answer, you're young and a little cranky right now, but we like you anyway.

B   If you chose this answer, you're older and a little cranky right now, but we like you anyway.

C   If you chose this answer, you're correct about freedom being a right. Unfortunately, it's not a reality for everyone on the planet. Maybe someday, when we get our global act together. Pray for that.

D   If you chose this answer, humbly thank God for making you wise. Since you're no doubt also cute and cuddly, thank God for that, too.

Chapter Two

Getting Away With It

___ Getting away with something that's wrong or not what it's supposed to be A) is the smart way to go through life if it makes your life easier or more fun B) is something real Christians never even think about C) is wrong D) is wrong, but it's such a common practice that it can't be *too* wrong	He who makes a fortune by a lying tongue is chasing a bubble over deadly snares. Proverbs 21:6 False scales are an abomination to the Lord, but a full weight is his delight. Proverbs 11:1

Maybe you live in a grass hut or an igloo that you constructed with your own hands, and you've lived there all your life. In that case, you may have trouble understanding this example.

But the chances are you live in a house or an apartment or a condo, and it's constructed from stuff like wood and metal and concrete and pipes and wires and shingles. Let's call it a house to make things simple. The important part is that you live in it—you and other people.

It has a foundation and the ground is supposed to be solid and level underneath it. No open places where the dirt was supposed to be filled in but wasn't. No cheating on the grade of cement.

But let's say that there are several places underneath your house where the dirt was supposed to be filled in, packed, and leveled, but—well, it wasn't. And let's say that the grade of cement the contractor used was the kind you use to patch holes in driveways, not the kind you use on foundations.

Why did the contractor do this? Because it was possible to get away with it. The contractor figured, "Why not?" and made an extra profit that way.

The framework of your house is wood—things called joists and studs and beams. Each one is supposed to be a certain thickness to support the house and keep it standing.

Let's say the contractor used thinner pieces of wood all over the house with the studs two feet apart instead of the standard sixteen inches.

Money was saved that way, and nobody was there to stop it. In other words, it was possible to get away with it. So again the contractor figured, "Use the cheap stuff, charge for the good stuff, pocket the extra profit. Nobody's looking—why not?" Similar things are true of the wiring and the roofing and the plumbing and the furnace and the water heater and the carpeting and the paint and the siding and—

Do you want to live in this place?

Maybe your answer would be, "For how long?" OK. For the rest of your life. Let's say this house is the only place you'll ever be able to live.

Call this house "society." Unless you're seriously into becoming a professional hermit, you will live in society all of your life. You'll spend your life going from one room in society to another. You will need and depend on what's in each room. You will hope that what is supposed to be there *will* be there.

It's also a two-way street. If you live in a house, you have to help maintain it. Now and then you need to change the furnace filter, clean the crud out of the gutters so they don't back up or fall off, check the oil in the car while it's in the garage to make sure the motor doesn't burn up, and wash the dishes so somebody's bacteria doesn't stay on a plate that somebody else will use in a little while.

What if you could get away with not doing some of those things?

What if you could just wipe the plates well enough with a paper towel so they look clean even though they're not? Would you?

What if you could *say* you checked the oil in the car, even though you didn't, but you knew people would believe you? If the motor burned out, you could always say there must have been a sudden leak somewhere after you checked it. Would you?

Once again, call the house "society." We will live here all our lives.

What if most of the people who build and maintain the house cheat on their responsibilities? What if most of the people simply make things look okay when they're really not? What happens to the house?

It becomes dangerous and, eventually, unlivable.

In a sense, each generation rebuilds society. Not completely from scratch, but somewhat. What kind of house/society do you want to live in? How safe, how reliable do you want it to be?

A decade or so ago, "Get real" was a standard part of young people's vocabulary. Most often it simply meant that the speaker disagreed with what someone had just said.

But "get real" or "be real" is pretty good advice. We need to give ourselves an occasional reality check. The key question is this: "Are the things I say and do real—honest, genuine, true, actually mine, everything they're supposed to be and everything I say they are—or are they usually simply whatever I can get away with?"

Your life, my life, our lives together: Is it what we truly accomplish, or is it what we can get away with? Is it something real that we do, or just a pretty good show we put on? Is it working and improving what we've inherited, or simply a matter of "beating the system?"

Your choice. But remember what happens to the house when the people who build it and live in it simply "beat the system."

"Why slave for hours when, with new Miracle Stuff you can get the same results in just minutes?" At the end, in tiny print few people notice, will come something like, "Results may vary."

"Pay no taxes—legally! Secret loopholes the government doesn't want you to know about! Send just $19.95!"

We're surrounded by advertisements like that—commercials for shortcuts. Now there's nothing genuinely wrong if a company really does make a spaghetti sauce just as good as Grandma's that you can simply heat up rather than spend hours making. (I challenge any such company, however, to a taste comparison with my mother-in-law's spaghetti sauce.)

But it's easy to pick up the idea that the secret of life is to learn how to make things look good without doing most of the work that makes them good, without having to deal with the truth, without being *real*. It's easy

15

to begin thinking in terms of, "Will this look or sound good enough?" rather than, "*IS* this good enough?"

Like all bad habits, what begins as a cobweb can become a chain, a routine way of thinking, a way of life.

For a while, shortcuts in the quality of our work or the honesty of what we say and do can seem like the clever answer to the responsibilities and challenges of living. It's similar to the way that alcohol or drugs can seem like the answer to boredom, stress, low confidence, or poor self-esteem. For a while, it seems to work.

But it's fake. It only *looks* okay. It only *appears* to be working. It's like an egg that's going rotten on the inside: you can make the outside pretty enough to win an award, but you still have a rotten egg. When the shell cracks, it's not pleasant to be around—whether you're watching and smelling the egg, or whether you *are* the egg.

It's a mistake to set up that situation by getting into a whatever-looks-good and beat-the-system way of looking at school, work, and life in general.

Being real is being like Jesus. Jesus was the perfect model of what we call "integrity," which literally means "being whole." Even people who didn't like him, even people who plotted his death knew that he was real, that there was nothing phony about him.

When you act that way, you like who you see in the mirror a lot better. And you're doing your part to make this house we live in all that it's supposed to be—both for yourself and for your kids. They will live here, too. Let's not bring them into a house where things look okay but are actually unreliable and dangerous.

"ANSWER" TO MICRO QUIZ

A You didn't *really* choose this answer, did you? Of course not. If you *had* chosen this answer, you would have needed to ask yourself if you wanted someone like yourself as a friend, neighbor, business partner, boss, or spouse.

B Well, maybe not Saint Francis or Mother Teresa. But most Christians are just plain tempted, and the possibility of getting away with something is part of the temptation.

C Yep.

D You might think differently if people routinely tried to shoot you.

Chapter Three

Teasing: Is It Really "Just a Joke"?

MICRO QUIZ

___ When you see cruel teasing going on, you should A) pray for the person who's being teased B) pray for the people doing the teasing C) organize a Christian vigilante posse to give those cruel teasers a really good taste of their own nasty stuff! D) other: _____	In everything do to others as you would have them do to you. Matthew 7:12 Truly I tell you, just as you did it to one of the least of these who are members of my family, you did it to me. Matthew 25:40

Imagine that a stray puppy wanders into your homeroom where you and your classmates are waiting for the morning announcements and for your homeroom teacher who is late.

The puppy is standing by the door, scared but sort of trusting. It's at the mercy of everyone there, looking around at them uncertainly.

Somebody gets up and slams the door shut. Immediately a few people get up from their seats, go to the front of the room, and surround the puppy. One of them gives it a shove in one direction, and another person shoves it back. They take turns leaning down and growling and screaming into its ears. They're amused by its whimpering. They chase it into a corner, poking at it with a yardstick.

The puppy is now a pathetic bundle of fear, cowering in the corner and trembling. Next, someone takes the meat from a packed lunch sandwich and holds it out to the puppy.

"Come on, little guy. We were just kidding, just having fun. It's okay. Come on out and have some breakfast."

17

The puppy is hungry. In spite of what just happened, it slowly comes toward the person holding the food. When it's almost there, that person yanks the meat away, roars at the puppy, pokes it with the yardstick, and sends it back into the corner, more terrified than ever. Everyone laughs.

Had enough? It's a pretty sick scene, so let's end it here.

If this actually happened in your homeroom or anywhere else, what would you do? Join in? Just watch and enjoy it? Wish it weren't happening but do nothing? Try to stop it?

What have you done in the past when something worse than this was going on and you were there? Like when the victim was not a stray puppy but a human being. A classmate.

You know them—the ones who are easy to tease, when it's easy for the teasing to get out of hand and into outright cruelty. The ones who are shy or overweight or weak or clumsy or different and, therefore, easy targets. The ones who can't afford the cool clothes, who never make the team or the cheerleading squad or the honor roll, and who never get invited to parties.

What have you done when people like that were backed into an emotional corner and the cool people (there are more accurate terms, but that's what they usually call themselves) were having fun with them?

Most people have no trouble understanding that tormenting a helpless animal is wrong, that it's outright jerk behavior. But crazily it's not so obvious when the victim is a person—even though that's a far worse action. Puppies may be cuter than some people, but people have far greater worth. Puppies are made in the image of parental dogs; people are made in the image of God.

There's a great range of teasing, of course, and not all of it is cruel. At one end is gentle, affectionate teasing that's actually meant as a compliment and a way of saying "We like you." At the other end, teasing is deliberately cruel, sometimes even deliberately planned.

In between are many shades of gray, including teasing that starts out harmless but somehow ends up hurting. It's like the case of two guys who begin trading punches in the shoulder, just a friendly exchange. Then one punch is thrown a little harder and hurts a little more than intended. Soon the exchange escalates until every punch is intended to seriously hurt. An exchange of words can build in the same way.

Sometimes teasing is intended to cause a reaction—a little emotional barb—but not great pain, yet for some reason the pain happens anyway. It's similar to opponents in a kung fu match, where the object is to score points with blows that hit but do not hurt. Sometimes one fighter doesn't pull the punch enough, causing serious even though unintended damage.

In both these cases, even though the hurting is difficult to catch and stop, it can always be apologized for—and should be.

And then there's teasing that arises from genuine verbal talent. Some people are good with quick insights and comments, often revolving around other people's characteristics or actions. They may be clueless about how much they really hurt the people who are the targets of their witty remarks. Unfortunately, a clever, witty remark seems to justify itself—to be okay just because it was clever and humorous.

Frequently these situations can be stopped before they get really painful through the action of somebody who's clearheaded enough to see what's happening. There's a big difference between butting into other people's business to meddle or control and stepping into their situation to keep someone from being hurt. We could use more people willing to do the second.

You, for example, the next time you witness something like this going on. That requires enough concern to care and enough courage to act on your concern. Both are qualities of real Christians.

Habitual teasing of the same easy targets, teasing that is deliberately intended to hurt, *is wrong.* Getting satisfaction and entertainment from causing pain is simply sick behavior. It's not true that anyone who does this is a totally sick jerk with no good inside whatsoever and deserves to be put in a cell with a psychopath. But the action itself—teasing deliberately to cause pain—yes, that's wrong and sick.

Few people want to be thought of that way. So people who bully others with hurtful teasing usually build up a small library of defenses and excuses to make their actions seem okay. Here are some of the usual ones.

"We didn't mean anything by it." This is nearly always a lie, even though the speakers may have convinced themselves otherwise. The teasing we're talking about *is* meant to have an effect on the target, and it's not to make that person feel okay.

"Everybody does it." This is probably the second most common excuse in the world. The most common is, "I couldn't help it." "Everybody does it" is used to excuse almost everything except bank robbery and hijacking alien spacecraft.

Most people go through life without being verbal bullies. "Everybody" here usually means "me and my circle of friends."

"It was just a joke." Also lame. A joke makes everyone laugh. People who get put down don't laugh. Not on the inside, anyway. They may fake laughter on the outside because that looks relatively cooler than bursting into tears. But they're not laughing because they found something funny in what was said or done.

"We were only having a little fun." Unfortunately, this is true. It's also exactly what makes it such jerk behavior. *Having fun* making someone feel lousy is incredibly cheap.

A word about the word *only* and its companion *just*. They're tied for first place in the Empty, Phony, Attempted–Butt-Wiping Words Competition. *Only* and *just* are routinely used to make something wrong somehow sound OK or at least not so bad.

"They're different, they're inferior, they're weird. They deserve it." People who use this excuse put themselves in the company of Adolph Hitler. It's the same one he used.

Why does anyone tease others hurtfully? If someone realizes that his or her teasing frequently hurts, knowing the "why" makes it easier to stop.

Some people tease others viciously simply because they're mean, nasty people. They weren't born that way and weren't always that way, but they are now. They've gotten a taste of inflicting pain, they positively like it, and they've become bullies and sadists. They don't want to change.

Low self-esteem is another common reason. That sounds strange because teasers act like they're in control of the world. But insecure people often make themselves feel better by controlling and manipulating easy-to-control people. It's similar to an alcoholic with low self-esteem who drinks to feel capable and confident. Taking a drink and putting somebody down can both become addictive.

And in both cases, the OK feeling doesn't last because it's not real.

That's why the behavior continues: another drink, another put-down— it's the same temporary band-aid. Feel OK for a short while, then feel empty, then repeat the action that makes you feel OK for a short while.

Some people hurt others with cruel teasing that grows out of displaced anger. At home or in another setting, *they* get verbally abused and put down. If they don't dare confront their own abusers, they may take out their anger on others who seem weaker.

I hope you're far more likely to observe harmful teasing than to do it. What if you see it going on in front of your eyes? What if you hear about it or see the results (like someone in tears in the classroom or on the bus), and you know the people responsible are your friends?

Tough situation, that's for sure. It invites the standard, safe response, "Not *my* problem." But recall the opening example of the puppy. Would you really stand by and do nothing, say nothing, if your friends were tormenting the puppy? Probably not.

So don't let it happen to a person, either. Don't wimp out on this one and let people hurt people right in front of your eyes while you watch. It's often said that the only thing necessary for evil to win is for good people to do nothing.

The situation calls for considerable Christian guts. You may have to temporarily risk your group status, put your coolness rating on the line. But if we never risk anything to act as a Christian, there's a good chance we have our faith comfortably stored in a closet somewhere to make sure it will never embarrass us.

Now if it's almost a rule of the group to make life miserable for people the group leaders don't like, then that group has social and spiritual cancer—and you need to get out. That kind of cancer is contagious.

But it may be that you see the harm being caused far more clearly than the people who are causing it. Maybe they'd stop if someone persuaded them to. Perhaps a dozen people, including you, would like to give that a shot but aren't sure how to go about it. Here are some suggestions that have worked for others.

First, change your mindset. Stop playing the safe, not-my-problem game. Be willing to take a risk.

You don't have to preach or come across as a dorky do-gooder. You don't have to point fingers and judge. You don't have to play a hero-to-the-rescue scene. Just deliver a simple, quiet message. "_____ has enough problems already. Why don't we stop giving him/her a hard time, OK?"

That gets agreement more often than you think. If it doesn't, don't get hot over it and turn it into a battle. Just quietly repeat the suggestion.

People who tease are not likely to say immediately, "We've been so wrong! We'll stop right now!" That doesn't mean they won't ease up later. They'd prefer it to look like their decision, not the result of your influence.

What if the teasing doesn't stop, if you really can't do anything to end it? You can still do many things to support the person who's being targeted. A sympathetic note, a phone call, a compliment, a few minutes of small talk. Anything to boost the spirit. It doesn't mean you have to become best friends.

There are a couple of extremes to avoid. First, if you offer help sneakily, making sure nobody could possibly catch you doing so, you're practically saying, "You are such a social zero that I can't risk being linked with you." That itself hurts.

On the other hand, don't turn your gesture of support into a fiery new allegiance that becomes a small war. ("*Yes!* former friends—I now support 'The Nerd!' And if you think I miss being with *you*, I never did like all of you very much anyway!")

Christians simply do not deliberately cause someone pain—or stand by and watch it happening. Remember the example; you wouldn't do that to a puppy. People are more precious than animals.

In the end, Jesus and everything he stood for will win over everything evil and negative. Join the winners ahead of time—make people feel good about themselves instead of bad. It's a much happier way to live.

"ANSWER" TO MICRO QUIZ

A Great idea. Also for yourself, to be given the grace of guts to do something.
B See response to A.
C You've been watching too many action-adventure, good-guys bad-guys movies.
D Yes! As for *what* other, well, the chapter did have a few suggestions.

Chapter Four

You Can Save a Life

___ When you celebrate your twentieth birthday, you will be A) twenty years old B) breathtakingly wise and mature C) celebrating this great event by reading over all your past World Cultures notes D) almost twenty-one years old	For it was you who formed my inward parts; you knit me together in my mother's womb. I praise you, for I am fearfully and wonderfully made. Psalm 139:13-14

Imagine this situation: The next few words that come out of your mouth will determine life or death for another human being.

Where or what would you have to be for this to happen? A military strongman in some corrupt dictatorship? A judge about to pass sentence on a serial killer? Could be, but you're not likely to end up as either one.

But the situation is real. If it happens, you're more likely to be at home in your room on the telephone with a friend or talking with a brother or sister. Or you're at a friend's house. Or in the parking lot after school.

The situation: Someone close to you is pregnant or has fathered a baby.

When they find out, they're not likely to run straight to Mom and Dad with the news. They'll go first to a trusted friend—maybe you. Never will they be more like putty in someone's hands or so dependent on someone's words.

They're in shock, confusion, anguish, and all the things that go along with, "I never thought it could happen to me!" Somewhere in this conversation they will ask the question, *"What am I going to do?"*

"My baby's life depended on who I talked to that day." That's how a young woman described the situation when she found she was pregnant by her boyfriend.

You may or may not be familiar with the facts about abortion. Here's a very brief overview. Since the 1973 *Roe v Wade* decision that declared state restrictions on abortion unconstitutional, a million and a half babies have been killed *every year*. Approximately four thousand abortions take place in the United States every day—an average of one every twenty seconds.

Ninety-eight percent of abortions are done for social or economic reasons. That means the baby is simply inconvenient, embarrassing, or financially burdensome.

Approximately one-third of all abortions in the United States are performed on teenagers. The baby will mess up the teen parents' bank account, education plans, career plans, social standing, and lives in general. So it's easier just to get rid of the baby.

Many people believe that abortion is legal only in the first three or four months of pregnancy. Actually, abortion is legal in the United States during *all nine months* of pregnancy. After the third month, some regulations may apply in some states. For example, the abortion may have to take place in a hospital rather than an outpatient clinic.

After the sixth month, the mother's "health" must be in danger for an abortion to be performed. But this doesn't mean the mother has to be in danger of death or disability. All she has to be is really upset over being pregnant. That's called a danger to her emotional or psychological health, and that counts. The baby doesn't.

Is "it" a baby? When the Supreme Court made its decision, the majority opinion declared that, "We need not resolve the difficult question of when life begins" and said that, since not all experts agreed, it could not provide protection for the unborn (for example, the right to live!) as it could for already-born people.

Yet even at the time, one medical expert after another testified that specifically human life *begins at conception*. Since then, the evidence for this has become even stronger.

A whole branch of medicine has developed to treat the unborn child as a patient. Delicate operations have been performed on unborn babies. Babies have lived and grown to be normal and healthy after being born at less than five months of the mother's pregnancy. Of babies born at only six months of pregnancy, 60 percent will live, and of these, 80 percent will be perfectly healthy.

Many abortions are performed at that stage of pregnancy and even later. So we have the following bizarre, insane situation: A baby is born two or three months premature. The baby is in an incubator to provide additional life support. A doctor who reaches into the incubator and slices the baby apart limb by limb would be tried for murder. A doctor who reaches into the mother's uterus *and does the very same thing* makes several hundred dollars.

By that reasoning, the only difference between a human being and a blob of matter is several inches—the distance down the birth canal. Outside, you're a person with constitutionally guaranteed rights. Inside, you're a blob of fetal tissue that can be legally disposed of if people don't want you around.

Why do doctors, who have sworn to preserve life, perform abortions? Many people—including doctors, nurses, and other medical personnel who used to perform abortions and have quit—say it's very simply the money. They've learned to tune out other considerations.

It's one of the highest-paying branches of medicine. An abortionist often makes considerably more money performing a day's schedule of abortions than a physician makes caring for a woman during her nine months of pregnancy and her delivery.

The procedures are fairly routine. Appointments are regular. No emergency calls in the middle of the night.

Teens make an especially easy mark for the abortionist's extremely profitable practice. A teen's unplanned pregnancy usually brings far more shock and confusion than an adult's.

Typical example: Jack and Jill, high school juniors. Nice kids from nice families. Regular, churchgoing people. Both have college plans.

And then, Jill gets pregnant by Jack.

Now into the situation comes the following message. It's given by someone who seems to understand, who frequently looks either like a young grandma or like a wonderfully caring Aunt Alice. She's sitting behind the desk at a clinic.

"Honey, we all make mistakes. And sometimes things happen to us that we just didn't plan. That's part of life, part of being a human being. But things like that don't have to ruin your future.

"You're young, you're talented, you have your whole life ahead of you. There's no need to let one mistake spoil all of that! One night versus your whole life? That doesn't make sense.

"It's so easy to take care of. I'm not telling you what to do, of course, but think of all the things you'd need to deal with. You're looking at years of responsibilities that you just don't have to accept until they're here, and right now they're not here yet. Maybe it's time to put the past behind you and get on with your life."

Doesn't that sound pretty persuasive? Even if you had opposed abortion in the past, doesn't that begin to sound kind of sensible…as though it just might be the way to go…in this particular case only, of course…even though it's sad and unfortunate…but…considering everything involved?

That's why girls who swore themselves against abortion when they sat in a classroom talking about it sometimes agree to one later anyway. Even though what they hear at the clinic is mostly a lie, it can make abortion sound like an unfortunate but perhaps necessary way out of a very and permanently complicated situation.

"They feel trapped, isolated, alone," says Jean Grigsby, of the right-to-life movement in Cincinnati, Ohio. "Abortion plays right into an idea that our culture promotes all the time—that there's a quick answer to all problems. On television, all problems get solved in thirty to sixty minutes. Abortion seems to follow that pattern—a quick, simple, easy solution."

But it isn't. Not long term.

The initial response is usually relief—just what abortion seemed to promise. *I can get on with my life!* Suddenly, after weeks of a black cloud hanging over everything, it's fun to go out and dance and be a teenager again. Shortly after this come denial and repression—kind of talking oneself into believing that it didn't really happen.

"That's especially easy if an authority figure, such as a parent, an older brother or sister, or a counselor promoted having the abortion," says Carla

McElhaney, director of WEBA (Women Exploited By Abortion) in Cincinnati, Ohio. "And it makes it easy to have a second and a third abortion. For a while, the first one feels like no big deal, so during that time a second or a third one is less threatening."

The relief, denial, and repression may be brief or may last several years.

"If the reality hits soon, the young woman is a bundle of raw emotions," Carla says. "But often she doesn't want to hear that healing takes time. Abortion promised a quick solution to a problem. Now she's looking for a quick solution to the pain of having had an abortion. But there isn't one."

In other cases, it can be five to ten or more years before the reality hits. "Often it's several years later, she's found the right guy, and she's pregnant with a baby that she wants," Carla explains. "Then she sees the pictures and hears the explanation of how a baby grows inside her—all the things they didn't tell her before. It's especially hard when she reaches the stage of pregnancy at which she previously had an abortion. Then it hits her: *If this time it's a baby, what was it the other time?"*

The answer, of course, is "A baby"—who was killed and gotten rid of.

What can you do if you're the one with whom someone shares the news of an unplanned pregnancy?

First, know the real facts about abortion.

This doesn't mean you could give a twenty-five minute speech about it on the spot. But know enough to be able to fight for the life of the unborn child and the emotional and spiritual life of your relative or friend.

You can get this information from a local right-to-life center. Two great pamphlets are available by mail or phone. One is *Facts You Should Know About Abortion* (Care Net, 109 Carpenter Drive, Suite 100, Sterling, VA 20164, 1-800-237-5030). A woman who, misinformed at age eighteen, chose abortion wrote the second one: *What They Won't Tell You at the Abortion Center* (Pro-Life Action Ministries, P.O. Box 75368, St. Paul, MN 55175-0368, 1-612-771-1500).

Second, listen and don't judge.

Let the fears and tears come. Hug. Then Jean Grigsby advises that you say, "Would you like me to go with you to tell your parents?" or "Let me be with you when you tell your folks." Having support there at the time can make a big, welcome difference.

Third, if your friend is literally unable to do that at the moment, go with her or him to a problem pregnancy center or pregnancy crisis center.

The names vary from city to city. Know where one is.

It should be a place where all services are free. Check that out. Abortion clinics sometimes use similar-sounding names, but services are not free.

Your friend needs to realize that, besides you, there *are* places and people to go to for help. Services include help with breaking the news to parents, counseling, medical help and prenatal care, maternity and baby clothes, even financial aid if necessary.

Fourth, don't forget to pray for your friend and for all the people involved.

God has a stake in this. Ask God to show you how to help.

It won't be easy for anyone. But killing is never the answer to a problem, including an unplanned pregnancy. It always makes things worse.

How many women do you suppose there are who wish they had never ended their babies' lives? If you're answering "millions," you're probably right.

How many women do you suppose there are who look at their two- or five- or ten-year-old child and think, "I wish I'd had that child aborted?"

"ANSWER" TO MICRO QUIZ

A Nuh-uh. When you celebrate your twentieth birthday, it's been twenty years since your *birth*. But that's not how old you are.

B Congratulations on your noble ideals. Let us hope they have indeed been realized. Just for the heck of it, you might want to check with someone and get a second opinion.

C If you chose this answer, you need to either
      —join a singles club composed of college professors or
      —refer yourself for therapy.

D Yes. On your twentieth *birth*day, you're actually twenty years and around nine months *old*. You were still you—and logging time—before the doctor and nurses nicely said, "Oh, what a *beautiful* baby!"

Chapter Five

Pornography: Cancer in Print and on Screen

MICRO QUIZ

___ Pornography is
A) produced on a pornograph
B) a not-very-nice but generally harmless part of any culture
C) a cause of suffering and destruction on an equal with drugs
D) something that might as well be tolerated because you're never going to get rid of it

> Everyone who looks at a woman with lust has already committed adultery with her in his heart.
>
> Matthew 5:28

> Your body is a temple of the Holy Spirit within you.
>
> 1 Corinthians 6:19

Fast-food restaurants are all over, right? There's seldom any problem finding one, no matter where you are. There's another retail business, though, that has *more outlets* than the largest fast-food chain.

Pornography. "Adult" magazines and videos. The buying and selling—and cheapening and trashing—of a gorgeous part of human nature called sex. Buying or renting bodies on paper or screen.

The *Final Report of the Attorney General's Commission on Pornography* is not the kind of book you pick up for quick, easy, or pleasant reading. In a way, it's more frightening than anything Stephen King has written. For example:

- The biggest audience for pornography is not dirty old men, but guys between the ages of fourteen and eighteen—precisely the age when attitudes toward sex and women are being formed. Most of the pornography produced, both magazines and videos, is eventually viewed by minors.

- The average first exposure to porn is between ten and twelve years old.
- Rapists are nearly always pornography users.
- Child molesters almost universally use pornography to stimulate their desires and, very frequently, to seduce the child.
- Pornography is an *eight- to ten-billion-dollar* per year industry. Approximately 85 percent of it is linked to organized crime.

"We warn and prepare our children for nearly everything else," says Phil Buress, president of Citizens for Community Values in Cincinnati, Ohio. "Cigarettes, drugs, alcohol, unplanned pregnancies, sexually transmitted diseases—everything but pornography. Somehow we don't want to see the danger in it or the possibilities for addiction."

Addiction to pornography is more common than most people think. Phil knows a lot about that, as he admits. "I was addicted to pornography for twenty years. It destroyed my first marriage and very nearly destroyed my life."

But let's not talk about actual addiction just yet. Let's start with a more common situation—a normal (meaning hormone-filled) and good young person (like you) with the opportunity to see a piece of pornography. It could be a magazine, a book, a video, or a late-night cable program.

It might be soft-core porn, like *Playboy* or *Penthouse*, or hardcore porn that graphically portrays everything from normal sexual activity to unbelievable perversions. Let's say it's not one of the latter. It's just you and a piece of porn.

Is there anything wrong, any harm done, if you spend some time with it? Some people would say no.

But if Jesus is anything more to us than a name and a nice idea, we have to consider what he said about it. "Everyone who looks at a woman with lust has already committed adultery with her in his heart" (Matthew 5:28).

He was not talking about the automatic appreciation and reaction to a body of the opposite sex—especially at a time of life when a square inch of opposite-sex skin seems to put a liter of hormones into Ready Alert Status. That's just being normal.

But deliberately soaking naked bodies and sexual activities in through your eyes for an extended period of time surely comes under what Jesus said. It also produces changes within us—gradual, perhaps, but real. Pornography takes scenes from our dark side and puts them in print or on film. It provides an indirect way of doing things we can't or won't—yet— do in person. Then we begin to conclude that it's okay…or almost okay…or at least not nearly as bad as we first thought.

Pornography can make even cruel sex look almost legitimate and normal. *Pornography tends to legitimize almost anything in the mind of the viewer.*

In a porn film that has been declared legally obscene over and over, a drugged, bound, helpless woman is sexually used in various ways by *five men* at the same time in front of an audience watching with enjoyment. It's a scene that ought to produce vomit and rage and tears for the pathetically abused, victimized woman. But I once heard that scene described as "pretty amusing—that's what I call coordination."

The speaker was not a warped and twisted pervert but a basically good person for whom frequent pornography, at that point in his life, had made even the massive sexual filth and horror of that scene almost legit or at least no big deal.

"What was your reaction the first time you saw real porn?" I asked him.

"You want to know the truth?" he said. "I felt like going out and raping somebody."

In a segment of *48 Hours*, Dan Rather commented, "More and more Americans are declaring war on all pornography. It's not just dirty, they say—it's dangerous." He was referring to another piece of legitimizing that pornography does—spreading the "rape myth."

The "rape myth" is the lie that women secretly want to be sexually used, even with force. They may protest at first, but once sexual activity starts, they find it pleasurable, even though it began and may continue with force and violence. A standard story line for many porn videos goes from "No, no!" to "Yes, yes!" to "More, more!"

"What would you say to a girl or a woman whose boyfriend was into pornography?" I asked Phil Buress.

Phil had answered my other questions in a calm, matter-of-fact tone of voice. This one prompted a response loud and intense enough to be heard out of his office and down the corridor.

"Run...*run*...*RUN!*" A few moments later, he added, "That's playing with fire. There's trouble ahead. Please take my word for it."

Does everyone who looks at pornography become genuinely addicted? Of course not, no more than everyone who sometimes gets drunk becomes a confirmed alcoholic. But people who are drunk or under the influence of any drug can cause great harm, whether they later become addicted or not. The same is true of people under the influence of pornography. And the influence doesn't stop as soon as the video is over or the magazine is set aside.

Dependence on pornography follows a pattern of five stages:

1. *Exposure.* This is the first few times of seeing the stuff. Usually the person just happens into a situation where porn is present. It doesn't mean this stage is harmless; recall the comment of the young man I quoted on page 32 about his reaction to first seeing pornography.
2. *Addiction.* The person deliberately seeks out pornography. Never in the world, however, would he consider himself addicted.
3. *Desensitizing.* Extremely graphic scenes that at one time might have disgusted or at least shocked him become accepted and easy to watch.
4. *Escalation.* Use of pornography now becomes more frequent. It now takes extremely graphic, explicit, or kinky activity to arouse excitement. "Regular" sex scenes that would shock most people seem almost boring.
5. *Acting out.* The user begins to do, at least in some way, what he has read or seen. Ted Bundy, a porn addict and perhaps the most infamous serial killer since Jack the Ripper, put it like this: "You reach that jumping-off point when you begin to wonder if actually doing it would give you that which is beyond just reading about it or looking at it."

This final stage doesn't always come quickly. There can be years between escalation and acting out, just as an alcoholic might be addicted for years before doing something disastrous as a result. Like most addictions, it's not always a nonstop escalation. Even before they get help, many alcoholics stop drinking for periods of time. Pornography addicts sometimes stop using it for periods of time, too.

Pornography producers and users defend it with lies.

• *"The First Amendment is at stake here! People should be free to watch whatever they want."*

Really? How about the sexual abuse and torture of children? There are people sick and evil enough to want to watch that.

"Well…maybe not *that*."

So the right to watch *"whatever you want"* does not exist. Where do you draw the line? People will argue about where it should be drawn, but anyone who says there is no line is dangerous. Producers of pornography love to invoke the flag, the First Amendment, freedom of speech, even patriotism. Then again, so does the Ku Klux Klan.

• *"But nobody's getting hurt."*

Tell that to the spouses and children of people who use pornography. (The top-selling video porn in this country is a series depicting incest.) Tell it to the former "stars" of porn movies who were drugged or threatened into appearing; who were so desperate for quick money that they agreed to it; who found during filming that the script called for more than they ever agreed to. Tell that to the victims of date rape by boyfriends who are into pornography.

The chapter "Victim Testimony" in the Attorney General's report is the saddest, most depressing thing I have ever read.

• *"You can't use people like Ted Bundy to make a case. After all, how many Ted Bundys have there been?"*

Only one, but quite a few others have come close. That's not the point. Few sex criminals reach that level and quantity of violence, but harm done by porn users is not a matter of unspeakable extremes versus no harm at all. Most hurricanes do not cause as much destruction as Andrew did a few years ago; does that mean other hurricanes are harmless?

- *"I still don't see any connection between pornography and behavior."*

Neither at first did Robert H. Macy, District Attorney of Oklahoma County, which contains Oklahoma City. But in 1991 he wrote, "The enforcement of the 1984 Oklahoma state law regarding the sale of obscene material has completely changed my opinion. Hard-core pornography acts on a person's mind much the same way as drugs."

His reason for changing his mind was simple: after the porn outlets were closed down, rape went down 27 percent! Macy called it "a dramatic reduction in the number of women and children who experienced the horrors of rape."

No connection between pornography and behavior? One of the finest young men I know came within an inch of joining in an evening of group sex with near strangers. This man has made many difficult decisions to act in a good and honorable way. I admire him. But for a while in his life, he was exposed to a lot of porn, including group-sex videos. Normally, he would have put group sex with strangers in the same category as robbing an armored car. *With* the influence of porn, he almost did it.

The day before Ted Bundy was executed in Florida, he said, "We [pornography users] are not some kind of inherent monsters. We are your sons, and we are your husbands. We grew up in regular families. Pornography can snatch a kid out of any home today."

It's unlikely that a few exposures to porn will turn you into a sex criminal. But do you want to take even a tiny step in that direction? Please don't start. If you have, please stop. Your future spouse and children don't deserve what can happen when pornography takes over.

In the Attorney General's report, Commissioner Diane Cusack wrote that pornography challenges one of those understandings held by society—that "sex is private, to be cherished within the context of love, commitment, and fidelity. We can use this wondrous gift to create or destroy, to rule or be ruled, to honor one another or debase one another."

It's a bad joke to call porn "adult" material. A mature person does not see people simply as body parts and nerve endings, as cheap toys to be used for temporary, often perverted thrills. Pornography does.

Don't take part in something that portrays people that way. Don't make one of the most beautiful parts of your humanity cheap and ugly.

"ANSWER" TO MICRO QUIZ

A If you chose this answer, you either have a sense of humor or a sense of cluelessness.

B Sure—harmless in about the same way as handguns.

C Yes. Doesn't get advertised that way, but in many people's opinion, yes.

D It's absolutely true that we'll probably never completely get rid of pornography. Of course, we'll never completely get rid of armed robbery, murder, and rape, either. Does that mean we should tolerate them?

Chapter Five and One Half (5 1/2)

Halftime

Author: This is great. We're halfway through the book, and you're still hanging in. We haven't even had any love scenes or car chases or—

Reader: You're going to have love scenes and car chases in a book like this?

Author: I like love scenes and car chases, along with the Loch Ness monster. Come to think of it, we can pick up on a scene I didn't finish in the book I wrote before this one.

Samantha's lips trembled as the helicopter, filled with organized crime hit men, descended closer and closer to the cab of the huge semi roaring down the narrow lanes of Route 47. Machine gun volleys whizzed past the window. Even so, her heart fluttered in appreciative awe as she watched Alexander's rippling, sinewy biceps wrestling the steering wheel of the massive vehicle. "Don't worry, Cupcake," Alexander said with a reassuring smile and a wink. "Two minutes and those guys are airborne toast." Then he risked revealing the softer, needing, vulnerable side of his masculinity: "Could you maybe have a kiss waiting?"
A quarter mile ahead on Route 47—

Reader: Excuse me, can we take a break?

Author: But we're almost at the part where Alexander—

Reader: Let me guess: He tricks the organized crime helicopter into flying into a cliff, and it explodes.

Author: How did you know?

Reader: Lucky guess. I think I'd just rather talk.

Author: OK. Well, what do you think of the book so far?

Reader: Way better than the unabridged dictionary.

Author: All *right!* That's the vote of confidence I needed.

Reader: Those people you mentioned in the last chapter—you said you knew them and you even quoted them—are they real, or did you just make up typical characters?

Author: They're real. In fact, I just played racquetball with one of them a few days ago. I don't make up typical real life characters to illustrate an idea. Seems fake. Besides, I've taught almost three thousand young people (some are really old now—in their late thirties, even), so I don't need to make anybody up. I know an awful lot of young people who are living the title of this book—*Real Life Takes Guts*. Some of them appear in the next chapter, by the way.

Reader: What's it about?

Author: Well…it, uh…uses the *s*-word.

Reader: You're kidding! *The s-word?*

Author: Yes. For mature audiences only.

Reader: Do you think I qualify?

Author: Did you tie your shoes all by yourself this morning?

Reader: Of course.

Author: You're in.

Chapter Six

To Be or Not to Be Sexually Active

MICRO QUIZ

___ Sex A) as far as I know, is simply the Latin word for *six* B) is strongly disapproved of in the Bible C) is holy D) is confusing	For this is the will of God, your sanctification: that you abstain from fornication; that each of you know how to control your own body in holiness and honor, not with lustful passion, like the Gentiles who do not know God; that no one wrong or exploit a brother or sister in this matter. 1 Thessalonians 4:3-6

"Hello?"

"It's me."

"Hi, Jack."

"Good news, Jill. I don't have to work tonight. How about a movie around seven?"

"Sounds great."

"How about pizza after the movie?"

"Sounds great."

"How about sex after the pizza?"

"Sounds great."

That's the picture some sources give of teenage and young adult behavior. They present a picture of relationships in which sex is nearly automatic, frequent, and cheap. That *does* happen *sometimes*—but definitely not always.

In fact, "nearly automatic, frequent, and cheap" is wrong on all counts. There are too many young people living and proving otherwise. They aren't heard from and written about often enough. You'll hear from some of them in a moment.

Whether or not to have sex—that's not a decision faced only by young people with no faith, no morals, and no conscience, young people who live in a moral sewer where selfishly satisfying sexual nerve endings is the only or main god.

There *are* people like that, of course, both young and old. For them the decision has already been made, and it's almost a nobrainer: *obviously* you do it whenever you have the chance and simply try to dodge any consequences.

At the opposite end, however, are many young people for whom premarital sex is out of the question. Their "no" is as automatic as other people's "of course."

But the whether-or-not-to decision confronts good, decent, fine young people. I've listened to and talked with hundreds of them. They reject cheap, let's-just-have-some-fun sex. But they've heard over and over that *"if you really love the person, it's okay."*

Is it?

No.

Does it make *any* difference?

Of course. Love makes it *not cheap.* That's quite different than selfishly using another person's body. But just because it's *not cheap* does not automatically make it right, good, smart, or consistent with God's plan.

There are three major flaws in the it's-okay-if-you-love-the-person idea.

- It's easy to *feel* in love for a while without genuine love actually there. Experience proves this over and over. You probably know people— including perhaps yourself—who felt cloud-soaringly in love for a while. But then the relationship rather quickly faded to nothing or blew up like a scene in an action-adventure movie. For a brief time, though, they were absolutely positive that this was real love that would probably last forever.

- Frequently a dating relationship does blossom into real love. It may not be the deep, mature love that grows over a long, committed period of time, but it's genuine.

  Problem is, this can happen many times. Child or high school sweetheart marriages still happen, but that's not most people's experience. Most people experience love several times before they find the person they want to marry. If you have sex every time you experience some degree of love, you bring an awful lot of sexual and emotional baggage from the past into your marriage, and that doesn't exactly help.

- It's possible to do some really stupid and even wrong things out of love. For example, I could use a brand new credit card to buy my wife a $7,000 diamond necklace because I love her. Giving her the necklace would be an act of love—and also an act of stupidity.

  A credit card might bring the necklace home, but we don't really *have* $7,000 to spend that way right now, and fifty million tons of love won't change that. Besides being irresponsible, it would be wrong because, with that kind of debt to repay, we couldn't buy things she *does* need more than a terrific necklace.

  When the right time comes, that necklace could be a beautiful and wonderful gift. Right now, it's a big mistake.

  Sex is often like that.

Many young people are rejecting the idea that sex positively belongs in a relationship and proves that you are both a normal and a caring person. I've talked with many of them and, with their permission, I will quote what they said. They're all real teens. I've changed only the names. What I quote is exactly what they said.

Terry, eighteen, and Beth, seventeen, have been an item for over a year, and the glances between them warmed the room as they sat at my kitchen table and talked about one of their favorite topics—each other. They get together or talk on the phone nearly every day.

"We want this to last," Beth said. "I guess that's not exactly unusual, but we think this is more than just going out."

"Are you planning a big wedding or just a small gathering of close friends?" I asked.

Terry rolled his eyes at my teasing but then grinned and admitted, "The idea *has* crossed my mind here and there. I think it would be…"

"Would be what?" Beth asked, obviously very interested.

"Pretty cool."

Until that happens, though, they've decided that sex will not be part of their relationship. Their reasoning goes like this: something may *feel* right but not *be* right, which means that sooner or later it's going to cause harm.

"We've seen that happen with friends," Beth said. "It seems like sex sort of takes over. It starts to run the relationship and sometimes ends up ruining it."

"It's been…a while since I was a teenager," I said, and then sang (sort of) a line from Elvis' "Hound Dog," which both Terry and Beth, God bless 'em, recognized from the local oldies station. "I understand how plain old hormones provide a lot of temptation, but that's not the whole picture. We've had adolescent hormones on the planet for thousands of years. As *you* see it, why are so many young people today sexually active?"

"I think people have been brainwashed into thinking that's the only way, or the main way, to show you love somebody," Terry said, "and that it's the only or main way you can have fun when you're with someone you like."

"They need a course in creative dating or something," Beth added. "There's millions of ways to have fun besides having sex."

Stacy and Greg, both in their late teens, are also very much in love and really want to stay together. That's why they made the decision, after several experiences, to *stop* having sex. They have a wonderful story to tell.

"Your experiences obviously weren't just cheaply using each other," I said. "What made you decide to stop?"

They exchanged glances and smiles. "Well, first of all it's the way we've been taught," Greg said after a small pause, "and it's really what we believe. But also because it *was* special. We could feel the power of it and how much it can mean. Now we want to save it so it'll be right and even more special when we make a permanent commitment."

"We don't ever want it to be ordinary, and we don't want any 'have to' in it," Stacy added.

I asked what the rewards were.

"We feel stronger, more genuine. We know that it's love holding us together, not sex," Stacy said.

What they're following is called *secondary virginity,* and it's a sign of a very strong and committed person. I asked some frank questions.

"Is it difficult?"

"Yes," Greg answered with an instant grin.

"A lot of your peers would probably say it's not possible to go back to just a nice warm cuddle."

"We wondered about that too," Stacy said. "But it *is* possible. We keep reminding each other of the promise we made to ourselves and to each other."

They share lots of hugs, compliments, talking, and listening. "This doesn't mean loving less," Stacy also pointed out. "We're actually closer because of this, and we can completely trust each other. We know there's nothing selfish in our relationship."

Again I played devil's advocate and asked for their response to the likely question, "Okay, but how much real fun is that?" Greg was again very direct.

"Well, fun is fun, but it can also be bad sometimes. We feel we're better persons for having control. If you can turn down something that's fun for reasons you know are right and good, that means more than having the fun."

"Any pressure or ridicule from peers who know of your decision?"

"My friends cheer me on!" Greg said. "Even the ones who *are* sexually active. They think it's great."

Stacy agreed. "A few people think it's strange, but my real friends respect my decision and admire it. They encourage me too."

That pretty well shoots down the nobody-will-think-we're-cool-anymore fear. Both of them assured me that there are far more virgin teens than anybody realizes. "They just don't get the publicity. People concentrate on the negative," Greg said.

Jane, eighteen, still hurts a lot over the breakup of a three-year relationship with her boyfriend. The relationship had been strong and stable enough that talk of marriage was not premature. And then...it's a long story. It wasn't exactly anybody's fault, but things completely fell apart.

"I'll always treasure the memories in a way," she said, "and it's hard to let them go. We had a lot of good times together, and we helped each other through a lot of bad times. We were good for each other. I wish it could have worked out, but it didn't."

She's grateful to her former boyfriend for one thing in particular. "He never pressured me for sex or for anything I didn't want to do. He was great that way. We had an understanding that we just weren't going to do that, and we kept it."

"And you're glad about that?"

"*Really* glad about that," Jane answered. "Not that I think it would have been horrible and ugly or something, but I always wanted sex to mean you're together forever. I still want it to mean that. Well, we're *not* together forever, that's for sure. It's hard letting go and starting over. If we had shared sex, I think I'd *really* be messed up."

If you're facing the should-we-or-shouldn't-we decision—or if you're having second thoughts about a previous "yes" decision—you should know that a lot of your peers are making a "no" decision work wonderfully well. They're having fun, and they're living free of guilt and consequences—two big obstacles to genuine happiness.

Which still doesn't make it easy; but it does make for genuine happiness.

Which is, come to think of it, the bottom line. A long time ago, a very wise man named Saint Thomas Aquinas said that: God made us for happiness.

Following the manufacturer's directions is always a good idea.

"ANSWER" TO MICRO QUIZ

A If you chose this answer, you're linguistically correct. *Sex* does mean *six* in Latin. You might also consider getting out more. Don't take that *too* far.

B Not exactly. In fact, not at all. The Bible is full of sex and approvingly so. Check out the Song of Solomon.

C Yes—along with every other human thing when it goes as God planned. And the holiness part does *not* cut back on the fun part.

D Also yes. People who have sex totally figured out either
   A)   are ten years old going on thirty or
   B)   should consider worrying about themselves a little

Chapter Seven

Bohemian Rhapsody in Real Life

___ Violence A) will probably always be with us B) will get worse and will soon make life almost unlivable C) can be decreased little by little if we really work at it D) is cool	Then Jesus said to [Peter], "Put your sword back into its place; for all who take the sword will perish by the sword." Matthew 26:52 Let us then pursue what makes for peace and for mutual upbuilding. Romans 14:19

"Mama, just killed a man. / Put a gun against his head, / Pulled my trigger, now he's dead, / Mama."

When Freddie Mercury first sang those lyrics almost two decades ago, did he know that the story in that strange, wonderful ballad would become a common opening paragraph in newspapers across the country? Probably not. But it has happened.

Freddie Mercury is dead now. So are many people who became victims of the kind of tragedy he sang about. Some of them weren't even born when he and Queen recorded "Bohemian Rhapsody." Violence, often unexplainable and called "senseless," has become a staple of life in too many places in our society, which likes to think of itself as advanced and highly civilized.

I'm glad that *Wayne's World* gave "Bohemian Rhapsody" a second life several years ago. It's a great song. But unfortunately most young people now associate it with the comic head-banging-in-the-car scene.

Wayne and Garth and company may have been on their way to a party at the time, but the story in "Bohemian Rhapsody" is no party—neither in the song nor in real life. It's not remotely a party for the victim, the attacker, or the families and friends who knew and loved each of them.

That's the tragedy of violence. It happens when people see other people as things, as objects to be used or hurt or wiped out, often just because they were in the way. "That person was just in the wrong place at the wrong time" has become a common comment about victims of violence.

But violence is never just a thing, an event that happened. Unless it's simply a case of someone beating a mound of dry desert sand with a baseball bat, violence is always about people. Violence is always a ripping, jagged gouge in the hearts of moms and dads and kids and grandparents and brothers and sisters and friends and husbands and wives and girl-friends and boyfriends.

What's your feeling about it all? Do you figure that somehow "they" will do something about violence? "They" seem to handle most problems that come up, right?

For example, if another country attacked us, "they" would do something about it and keep us safe, right? After all, when streets get potholes, "they" fix them. When a little kid falls in a pool and almost drowns, we call 911 and "they" come and save the kid who's at the brink of death. Sometimes it even gets dramatized later on TV.

So even though we may have to go through a few more years of this violence stuff, "they" will somehow fix it. That's what I hear when I talk with young people about violence.

But maybe it won't work like that.

Maybe your generation will have to fix it.

"They" can make new laws, build more prisons, raise money for new programs. But those things are often band-aids. Band-aids can temporarily keep a wound from getting worse; they can make the wound look more respectable on the outside. But they can't wipe out the infection. That has to happen from the inside.

47

You're the generation with a chance to change things from the inside, to turn things around from the source. In many ways, the kind of world your children and grandchildren will live in is up to you.

You *can* make a difference. Please believe that. You can make a dent in the statistics on rape, robbery, assault, and homicide. If you're thinking, "What's one little dent?" remember that even one less act of violence means someone will be whole and healthy rather than scarred and wounded and suffering; perhaps it will mean someone is alive rather than dead.

Here are some things you can do.

1) *Resensitize yourself to violence.*

Be upset and bothered by violence. Action for change happens when people feel something strongly.

Being upset and bothered isn't difficult if it's a family member, neighbor, boyfriend, girlfriend, or classmate who gets shot, raped, or assaulted. Obviously you won't get those same intense feelings from reading a newspaper story or listening to a TV news report. But don't put it on almost the same level as sports scores or movie reviews.

Convince yourself that violence is not glorious or cool, no matter how it's portrayed. Movies in particular can desensitize people even to the horror of extreme violence.

That doesn't mean a film should never portray anything nastier than people making faces at each other. The true horror of the Holocaust could not be portrayed without some graphic scenes.

But some of those scenes brought laughter and applause from a group of students watching *Schindler's List*. That's frightening.

Did the laughter come from raw anti-Jewish prejudice? Maybe. But I think that more likely it came from exposure to bodies being sliced and blown apart on movie screens in ways that made the action look like games and people like things.

2) *Don't get caught up in the circle of violence.*

If that sounds like obvious advice you don't need, remember that becoming involved in violence happens by degrees. Very few people wake up in the morning and say, "Today I'm going to join a gang and trash something or somebody."

Hanging around occasionally with gang people, official or unofficial, is a start. At first it brings the thrill of just being on the fringe of something dangerous and the semistatus of associating with dangerous people. But that can quickly get bumped up to "If you want to hang around with us, you've got to be one of us," which means doing what they do and hating the people they hate.

Investing in a weapon of any kind and taking it with you is another first step toward tragedy. It can seem like an unfortunate but necessary thing to do: "With some people around here the way they are, you gotta have something to defend yourself with."

Problem is, you never hear or read stories of teenagers successfully defending themselves with a knife or a gun against an attacker and the authorities saying, "Good thing the good kid had a weapon to use on the bad kid."

But you hear lots of stories of kids who, in a tight situation, reach for a weapon they never really intended to use—and pay for it for years and years to come.

I remember a newspaper photo of an eighteen-year-old a few seconds after he received twenty years to life for murder. His handcuffed hands are clenched together against his mouth, his eyes already have the imprisoned look of someone gazing out from behind bars, and he's beginning to cry. He's not tough anymore. Just scared and helpless.

> "Mama, life had just begun. / Now I've gone and thrown it all away."

3) *Wrap yourself around something good and positive and don't let go.*

"Mama, just killed a man." Freddie Mercury's lyrics don't mention a specific reason for pulling the trigger. But listen to the lines that precede that one.

> "Easy come, easy go, / little high, little low, / any way the wind blows / doesn't really matter to me."

49

Maybe that sounds like a cool, unattached, nicely laidback lifestyle: don't take anything too seriously, don't get tied down, and don't invest too much of yourself in anything. Just drift on and assume that everything will turn out okay.

It's also a recipe for disaster and sometimes tragic violence.

People don't usually think well or live well on a mental diet of

> "Easy come, easy go...any way the wind blows / doesn't really matter."

That's called having no values, no foundation, and no connection to anything.

Again, not being connected to anything can seem like a formula for freedom. But more often it's like being in a small, light airplane in a heavy windstorm. It isn't connected to anything either, and it doesn't have much substance on its own. It's going to get tossed around a lot and may not make it.

We need connections. We need spiritual stakes in the ground to keep us from doing something stupid when the winds of tough situations get rough.

What connections to make? Check in with Jesus.

4) *Reach out with kindness whenever you see a chance.*

Violent actions don't always come from people who are routinely violent by nature or by positive decision. They often come from people who later are described by friends and neighbors as "nice," "friendly," sometimes even "helpful" and "kind." So what happened?

Often something inside that most people didn't see boiled over. If only there had been a valve that could have relieved the pressure, things might have been different.

Maybe you could be one for someone who needs one. True, that's not a glamorous description. ("And what do you like to do in your spare time?" "I enjoy being a pressure-relief valve.")

Is there a classmate who's on overload with family problems and seems just plain angry and hopeless about everything? No, you can't be his or her professional counselor or therapist, but you can make a phone call, write a note, or offer to listen. And when you listen, don't just agree that everything is truly lousy and hopeless.

If you feel it's needed, take a risk and add something direct and honest like, "Please don't do anything stupid, okay? Lots of us like you too much to see you get messed up."

You'll probably never know what you may have prevented. But anytime you reduce anger and hopelessness in another person, you cut down on the likelihood of violent behavior.

5) *Prepare to build a strong family.*

I remember a headline that read, "Juvenile crime up sharply—love, self-worth, family support lacking."

Sure, there are no guarantees. But when a kid has two adults who give love, support, guidance in knowing right from wrong, and a feeling that he or she is worth something, there's dramatically less chance that this kid will grow up and stick a knife in someone's body or put a gun to someone's head.

What will things be like when your kids are growing up? A big part of it depends on the kind of marriages you make, the kind of families you build.

A few years ago, a Senate panel listened to a report on rising teen pregnancy. Single (and often unsupported) mothers now account for nearly 70 percent of babies born to women under twenty years old.

Are all those babies doomed? Let's hope not. But do they have a much greater chance of growing up in the kind of rootlessness and poverty that breeds violence? Dumb question.

Senate subcommittees can make recommendations and design programs, and that's fine, but they won't really change anything until your generation wants changes badly enough to make them happen, until young people decide, "No, this *isn't* okay; it's tearing us apart."

"Perhaps the greatest social service that can be rendered by anybody to the country and to mankind," George Bernard Shaw said, "is to bring up a family."

"Mama, didn't mean to make you cry."

If you can keep just one incident like that from happening, the world really will be a better place.

"ANSWER" TO MICRO QUIZ

A   Probably so. So? Let's hope that doesn't mean we just accept it.

B   If someone really believes this, ask him or her, "Are you going to bring kids into that world and leave them on their own to try to survive, or are you going to try to change things?"

C   Yes. Yes. Let's look for ways to start.

D   Would you still say this if your daughter had been robbed, beaten, or raped?

Chapter Eight

Is It All Phony?

_____ The word *phony*
A) is a version of *phooey*, meaning, "I don't buy it"
B) comes from the Greek word *phonos* which means *sound* and is used for things that sound different from what they are supposed to be
C) usually describes stuff you get Phor Phree
D) would be a good word never to have to use, especially about yourself

If a brother or sister is naked and lacks daily food, and one of you says to them, "Go in peace; keep warm and eat your fill," and yet you do not supply their bodily needs, what is the good of that?
James 2:15-16

In a live interview, Bobo Mammoth announced his upcoming match with Madman Gutcrusher. It's a title match and a grudge match, with the Intergalactic Federation of Wrestling Heavyweight Championship at stake. A few months ago, Bobo had the championship stolen from him when Madman Gutcrusher used help from an alien life form (it was purple and about the size of Madman's manager) to win the match. The alien swung down into the ring and put Bobo to sleep with an extraterrestrial crystal. By accident, the referee didn't see it, so he awarded the championship belt to Madman.

Reactions?

"That stuff is *so* fake."

"That's professional wrestling, not *real* wrestling."

"It's all phony."

True, the story line and outcome of the matches are probably scripted long before the opponents step into the ring. But is it phony? That depends on what you expect professional wrestling to be. You may think it's stupid entertainment, but it's phony only if it's guaranteed to be a real athletic competition where the outcome is still to be decided.

Most people realize it's a staged show. They don't expect it to be real any more than they expect the actress playing Juliet actually to kill herself with Romeo's dagger.

How about these situations?

- *Holiday closeout sale on every diamond and piece of gold in stock! All items 60 to 80 percent off!*
- *Designer fashion-wear ensembles: Were $159.95—now $49 to $79!*

This is more serious than professional wrestling. True, many people reading those signs automatically think, "Right. If they actually sold merchandise for that much off its true value, they'd go bankrupt and close business next month."

But others may actually think that a discount like this will never happen again, it's the opportunity of a lifetime, and they'd better get right out to the store and buy now before the opportunity is gone forever. Which, of course, is the reaction the advertisers had in mind.

Is that phony? You could make a decent case for it here. But even when we see through it, it doesn't bother us a whole lot. Most of us feel equipped to see through and deal with advertising gimmicks. Sometimes we even get a laugh out of too-good-to-be-true advertisements.

But other kinds of phoniness aren't laughable at all, and they're in the headlines a lot these days. The media love them. We read about police chiefs indicted for receiving stolen goods. We hear about county commissioners prosecuted for embezzlement. We see senators accused of accepting campaign contributions from people who want political favors.

Investigative reporters for newspapers and television have dug up dirty laundry on just about every kind of public person and institution. When we discover a big gap between the outside and the inside of someone or something, that's upsetting. These are people and institutions we're supposed to be able to look up to and trust.

One easy way of dealing—or rather not dealing—with it is to conclude

"It's all phony. Politics, business, church, school—everything. It looks good on the outside but on the inside it's all rotten and full of crooks."

That's sad. More than sad, it's wrong, and it hurts people.

• *Everyone in a certain category comes under automatic suspicion.*

A senator is accused of shady dealings, and people assume that most of the other ninety-nine are doing the same thing but just didn't get caught. A youth leader is accused of abusing kids, and suddenly any youth worker who puts an arm around a crying twelve-year-old is under suspicion.

That's monstrously unfair and wrong. Try it on. Pick a role that you fill. Perhaps it's teenage babysitter. If another teen is caught stealing from the home where he or she works, would you like being under suspicion simply because you have a similar job? If a teenage athlete is caught using steroids to boost performance, would you like being suspected of doing the same thing just because you're also a teenage athlete?

"If there's a few bad ones, most of 'em are probably bad" is terrible logic and a morally unfair view of people. This is what happens as a result:

• *Hope for making things better drains away.*

"You can't fight the system. The crooks are in charge. You can't change it."

When we believe that, even a little, an attitudinal black hole opens up and begins swallowing and destroying the talent and motivation that could have made things different and better.

"It's all phony, it's all a big game" can become an easy way out of the effort it takes to belong, believe, try, work, and hang in. Why pound at a concrete wall with your bare hands?

There *are* such things as concrete walls in life. But seeing every fault, every problem, and every needed change as a concrete wall that you may as well accept—that's called giving up. Father Andrew Greeley once pointed out that "Hope demands effort. Despair does not." If enough people begin to think, "Why try?" then the saying comes true that the only thing necessary for the triumph of evil is for good people to do nothing.

• *The temptation grows to give in yourself—a little here and there.*

Few people make an absolute decision to specialize in professional hypocrisy. But "Everybody does it" is tempting. "What difference does it make whether I pass by learning or by cheating? The teachers probably cheated when they were in our place."

The voice that used to say "Be real, be your own best self" gets weaker and finally is silent. In sometimes a very short time, all that matters is that things look OK on the outside.

There's some phoniness in any group, from classroom committees to worldwide organizations. Demanding that every person or group be perfect or else you'll quit and withdraw your allegiance and effort is arrogant and stupid. It's like saying, "They have to be perfect to be worthy of me."

Life is a mixed bag, as Jesus pointed out long ago in his parable of the wheat and the weeds (Matthew 13:24-30). Unfortunately, weeds make most of the headlines. Print and television magazines feature more weed stories than wheat stories.

It would be nice to see some wheat headlines now and then:

SPOUSES REMAIN FAITHFUL AND IN LOVE FOR DECADES

PROSECUTOR REFUSES DEAL WITH UNDERWORLD CRIME BOSS

PARENT FORFEITS PERSONAL INTERESTS TO CARE FOR CHILDREN

CAR MECHANIC CHARGES FAIR PRICE FOR MINOR REPAIR. "THE RATTLE SOUNDED MORE LIKE $500 THAN $17.50," SAYS GRATEFUL OWNER.

Your job is to see the wheat of the day—the times when people were real and good and loving. Fields of wheat are seldom announced by blaring trumpets or lit up by strobe lights. When you learn to see the wheat, you'll know where Jesus is hanging out these days.

"ANSWER" TO MICRO QUIZ

A No. *Phooey* is an ancient, mild cuss word used by students who were not prepared for their final exams.

B No. Things that sound different from what they're supposed to are called "karaoke."

C Real phunny.

D Yep.

Chapter Nine

Too Cool Not to Care: Confronting a Friend

___ Before confronting a friend who's into some bad stuff, you should A) learn kung fu B) wait and see if it really harms them C) organize a committee to study the problem D) pray	My brothers and sisters, if anyone among you wanders from the truth and is brought back by another, you should know that whoever brings back a sinner from wandering will save the sinner's soul from death and will cover a multitude of sins. James 5:19-20

"I don't think I could be a teacher," an old friend and high school classmate remarked to me over lunch one time.

"I agree," I said solemnly. "You seldom did your homework, so you'd probably feel really guilty about assigning some. There's also this thing called actually reading the textbook."

It wasn't completely true, but it made a decent friendly insult, which is a technique guys use to say they understand and like each other. After a few further comments, which we don't need to quote exactly, he said, "I mean, doesn't it get to you when you see a kid start to get messed up or hear about it?"

"Sure. It bothers a lot of *them*, too."

"What do you mean?" my friend asked.

"Just that. It's amazing how many teens hurt when they see a friend make some bad decisions and start to go down the tube."

"How do you know?"

"They say so. They tell me."

"So what do you tell them?"

"Depends. Sometimes that's when I wish I'd gotten into plumbing instead of teaching."

"Great career for you, Jim," he said, "except there's this thing called knowing a pipe wrench from a faucet."

Most young people have dreams that are amazingly similar: find someone special to love who will love you back; bring some kids into the world who will love you and make you proud of them; find a career you like that pays enough to buy some decent things; live in a nice place; feel good about your life and what you've done with it.

Along the way come variations that include being a star in the NFL or the NBA; careers in science, the arts, or construction; and adventures of all kinds across the globe. But the bottom line is the same: achievement, happiness, and peace with people you love and who love you.

Nobody deliberately changes that dream to, "When I reach my late twenties, I want to have about three unplanned and mixed-up kids by two or three out of the eight or ten sexual partners I've had. It would also be cool to have my career plans go down the toilet. An alcohol or drug problem might be neat, too. Also I'd like to have dropped all my old friends and hang around with the kind of people everybody warns you about."

But sometimes you look at one of your friends, and you'd almost swear that he or she had made exactly that decision. In the space of a school year or less—sometimes a couple of months—your friend seems drastically changed. Yet in spite of a lifestyle almost certain to blow the dream apart, he or she somehow still expects to get there. It leaves you feeling hurt, abandoned, betrayed, sad, angry, frustrated, and worried. And wishing you could do something.

Should you try? Will it work?

If you're looking for instant and dramatic results from your efforts, this may not be the place to look for them. But, yes, it can work.

You have to decide you *want* to do something. That sounds a little simplistic, but many things go undone because people never decide definitely to do them. The idea gets filed in a mental "Maybe If A Chance Comes" land. Almost everything that gets filed there dies there.

This doesn't mean you drive into your friend's life at the first available moment like an army tank on a liberation mission, all guns firing. It means you decide definitely to take the risk of trying to help.

And it's definitely a risk. Could you lose? Not in the long run, because no act of kindness and love will ever come out a loser when this whole cosmic ball game is wrapped up. God has guaranteed that.

But in the meantime you could be in for some misunderstandings and further frustration. You should know that going in. Remember that it's also possible things may work out spectacularly.

There's a dark side to trying to bring a friend back from a potentially destructive lifestyle. A desire to help a friend can grow into an obsession, a monster that overtakes your life, consumes you, and destroys your own peace. Almost nothing else matters, for a while anyway, besides getting the person to change. That isn't healthy for you, and it could make you come across like a fanatic who's gone off the deep end—which hurts your credibility.

When you're trying to help a friend come back to his or her senses and give up a headed-for-trouble lifestyle, it might seem as though there are a dozen or so things you can do, and if you just locate the right one, success is guaranteed.

Not so, unfortunately. There are basically three things you can do.

1) *Confront the person.*

There's a difference between waiting for the *guaranteed perfect* moment to talk (that almost never happens) and waiting for a good moment. A good moment can happen when your friend seems a little more like his or her old self, when you're sharing and doing things that characterized your friendship in the past. If one of those moments doesn't drop into your lives, try to encourage it without forcing it.

What to say?

Not any of these: "You've turned into a real jerk." "You're being totally stupid." "You're throwing your life down the toilet like a _____ idiot."

"You used to have some brains and common sense. I think your new friends sucked them all out of you."

I know, it's tempting—especially if you're really angry about the way your friend is acting. But these things come with an Almost-Certain-to-Blow-Things-Up-and-Make-Them-Worse Warranty.

A better mix of what to say includes four main items. You can say them in your own way.

- I'm really concerned about you because I think what you're doing will harm you. You're important to me, and I don't want to see you get hurt.
- This doesn't mean that I think you're terrible, and it doesn't mean I think I'm superior. It means just what I said: I'm concerned about where you're headed.
- If you're angry with me (there are more colorful ways of saying this) and think I'm butting into your life, I'll understand, but that won't change my belief or my concern for you.
- If you need me, I'll be here.

In other words, it's pretty much what God would say, which is why God often sends friends to people in trouble, to talk for God—which is the actual meaning of the word *prophet*.

You're not likely to hear immediately, "My gosh, you're right! I see it so clearly now. I'm going to completely reverse my behavior before it kills me—and I have you to thank!"

You're more likely to hear something like, "You're worrying over nothing. I know what I'm doing, and I can handle myself. Besides, it's my life."

Prophets are seldom greeted with instant success; check the Bible. You have to trust that your message of concern will have some effect sometime, even though you may not see it.

2) *Enlist adult help.*

On a scale of scariness, this ranks on a level with facing a pack of snarling Dobermans. It violates the Ultimate Unwritten Code of Law for the age group.

But it often works. Here's a true example.

"There's only one thing you can do," I told a girl once. She had asked me what she could do to help a friend who had fallen back into abusing alcohol and drugs. He hadn't kicked the lifestyle; he'd just gotten more clever about covering it up.

"You've talked to him and he tunes you out, right?"

"Right."

"Other people have talked to him too?"

"Right."

"There's only one thing left. You have to tell his parents. You have to get them in on it. They're the only ones with the leverage to make something happen."

It wasn't what she wanted to hear. We talked about how much courage it would take. I asked her if she felt up to it. She said yes, and she followed through—under almost the worst of circumstances.

Her friend was supposed to be at work late the following afternoon while his mother was at home. She called. *He* answered. His work schedule had been changed.

Many people would have made up a sudden, phony reason for the phone call and postponed the job of talking to his parents.

She didn't. She asked for his mother, delivered her message, and waited for the ugly fallout. No possibility of remaining anonymous now. She expected to be thoroughly hated, cussed out, and badmouthed, and that's what happened.

The unexpected and wonderful part is that it lasted only two days. Then he thanked her, and now he's extremely grateful.

They don't all end that way. Sometimes the waiting period between anger and thanks is closer to a couple of months or a couple of years than a couple of days. And sometimes it never comes. If you take the risk in spite of this, you prove yourself a true and very strong friend.

3) *Turn it over to God.*

Unfortunately, this can sound like a last resort when it should be the first!

"Nothing we tried is working. The situation is probably hopeless, but hopeless situations call for last-ditch, desperation, one-chance-in-a-million measures—so let's give God a shot at it." Not intelligent.

It's tempting to think that there's always a perfect thing to say or do if we could find out what it is. If we could find the right button to push, we could bring anyone back from stupid stuff he or she was doing.

But life isn't that simple, and people aren't that mechanical. They're not motors that can be repaired and made to run smoothly if you just find the part that's messed up. Sometimes you just have to let go and tell God, "This one is yours to handle."

That's not easy. We want to feel in charge, and we usually want very quick results. Turning things over to God means giving up being in charge and accepting God's time schedule. But it doesn't mean backing out of the picture.

It means we hang in through prayer. Not an easy, one-time, no-effort prayer either: "Dear God, please help _____," and then we're out of there and off to other things. Some situations call for lots of prayer.

Why? Well, it's not to change God's mind and persuade God that this person is worth caring about. God knows that going in.

So why pray? Good question. Often it's through repeated prayer that *we*, not God, are changed and finally see what to do.

Still, we don't know exactly how prayer "works." In fact, the best way of making sure you'll almost never pray is demanding to know how prayer works and exactly how much of it is needed to produce certain results. Prayer is an act of hope and trust, not an exercise in button pushing.

Finally, prayer is not just something to turn to when all other options have failed. It's something to do *before* you try anything else. God has a huge stake in the future of the friend you're concerned about. God belongs in your helping venture from the very start.

"ANSWER" TO MICRO QUIZ

A) Not a bad idea, *if* your friend is exceptionally bad tempered and you can master kung fu from watching a thirty-minute video.

B) Bad idea. By the time you have globs of concrete evidence, the damage is already done.

C) No. However, if you chose this, you have a potentially great career in government.

D) Yep.

Chapter Nine and One Half (9 1/2)

A Final Conversation

The organized crime helicopter bounced off the cliff and exploded merrily. "Check the sideview mirror, Cupcake," Alexander said to Samantha with a grin. "There's a pretty good fireworks show back there."

"You did it," Samantha purred as Alexander braked the huge semi down to ninety miles per hour. He looked at her. Never had she been more beautiful. She looked at him. Never had he been hunkier. He leaned toward her. She leaned toward him. The air between them in the cab became electric at the approach of their kiss. In fact, even the air all the way back in the storage compartment was—

Reader: Excuse me, can I go get something for my nausea?

Author: Just thought I'd finish the car chase-love scene before we end the book. I'm getting to like writing them.

Reader: I'd rather be kept in suspense.

Author: Your choice. Well, this is it. The book's over.

Reader: I guess you want to know what I think of it.

Author: That's always on a writer's mind, but it's difficult to find out the truth, so I seldom ask. If someone *gave* you the book for some occasion, instead of giving you a Bermuda vacation or a Porsche, I hope you don't hold it against them.

Reader: Of course not. Who would want a Porsche when they could keep driving their '83 Buick *plus* own your book?

Author: It's getting a little thick around here.

Reader: Any final thoughts? I guess that's what this chapter 9 1/2 is for.

Author: Exactly. Well, remember the dream I talked about in chapter 9? I hope you make it happen. You deserve it.

Reader: How do you know that? I mean, I agree, but—

Author: You made it through the book, didn't you? That took guts and deserves a big reward right there. More seriously, I'd like to ask you something. Can you blink your eyes?

Reader: Yeah. All by myself, too.

Author: Good. That means you're *alive* and you're *here*, and *that* means you deserve the dream. This isn't just my idea, by the way. It's God's, but I heartily agree with God—that's always a pretty good move, by the way, if you want a little extra golden hint. It'll take some work on your part to help make the dream happen, though. Don't let anybody or anything undermine it.

Reader: Anything else?

Author: Keep checking in with God. Ask God for direction and mean it. And then listen. That can be a difficult and scary thing to do sometimes. I think that about wraps it up. Wish we could meet in person.

Reader: Why?

Author: I could teach you how to wax the car, mow the lawn, paint—

Reader: Didn't you say "Get real" back in chapter 2?

Author: Yeah. Okay, we could play racquetball and have lunch. But in case that doesn't happen, hang in. I'll pray for you, by the way.

Reader: How can you pray for me when you don't know who I am?

Author: Don't have to. God knows. God's the connection. It's pretty cool, actually.